Mark H. Hoeksema

Studies in
HEBREWS

REFORMED
FREE PUBLISHING
ASSOCIATION
Jenison, Michigan

Scripture cited is taken from the Authorized (King James) Version

Reformed Free Publishing Association
1894 Georgetown Center Drive
Jenison MI 49428
616-457-5970
www.rfpa.org
mail@rfpa.org

Book design and typesetting by Erika Kiel

ISBN 978-1-944555-28-3
LCCN 2017959446

Introduction

The epistle to the Hebrews is one of the most difficult books of the Bible to interpret. Yet it is important to study, primarily because it helps us to understand the relation between the Old and New Testaments. Those who sometimes struggle with the interpretation, but nevertheless persevere will find in Hebrews the rich fruit of learning and edification.

The Time and Place of Hebrews

Neither the time nor the place of the writing of the epistle can be known with certainty. It is generally agreed among biblical scholars that the date of Hebrews is between AD 50 and AD 70. No one knows for certain where it was written, although Italy is a possibility (Heb. 13:24).

The Writer of Hebrews

The Holy Spirit is the author of Hebrews. The identity of the human writer whom the Spirit was pleased to use to author Hebrews is unknown, despite the heading of the book in the King James Version of the Bible as "The Epistle of Paul the Apostle to the Hebrews." This heading must be ignored, since it is not inspired and is, in fact, inaccurate. Many have thought that Paul was indeed the author, especially the church during the long period of the Middle Ages, although the early church did not think so. The evidence against Pauline authorship is overwhelming and convincing. The end of the matter is that the writer's identity is unknown. If God had wanted us to know who wrote the epistle, the Holy Spirit would have told us.

The Addressees of Hebrews

The generally accepted date of Hebrews is important because it confirms that the epistle was written to Jewish Christians who were recent converts to the faith. In obedience to the divine command, the apostles had preached the gospel first to the Jews and then to the Gentiles. Undoubtedly, Jews were a large percentage of the early New Testament church, which accounts for the fact that the epistle speaks primarily to the children of the Old Testament. Some have attempted to narrow the scope of Hebrews to specific groups of Jews, but there is no good evidence to substantiate this idea. It is instead correct to assert that the epistle was written to the Jews of the dispersion and by extension to the Gentile Christians as well.

The Theme of Hebrews

The main theme of Hebrews is the relation between the Old Testament and the New Testament. The transition from the Old Testament structure of types and shadows to the New Testament economy of reality was not instantaneous or even swift, but slow and gradual. The Jews were understandably unable to make the transition from the age of types to the day of reality. The writer therefore instructs the church concerning the relation between the old and new dispensations. The relation is not one of dichotomy or of essence, but that of fulfillment.

Two subthemes present themselves. One is the concept *better*, a term used twelve times in the epistle to help define the relation between the testaments. For a correct understanding of Hebrews, it is essential to remember that the two dispensations are not essentially *different* from one another, but that the new is *better* than the old. This also explains why the writer of Hebrews quotes the Old Testament fifty-two times from thirteen different books; the writer emphasizes the idea that the new covenant is the fulfillment of the old throughout the book. There is only one covenant from Genesis 1 to Revelation 22, although with ever-clearer manifestation and development. This increasing clarity the writer traces in terms of a better testament.

The other subtheme is the emphasis on faith as contrasted with sight (2 Cor. 5:7). This theme runs throughout the epistle and is particularly evident in the classic chapter 11, which highlights the beautiful faith that was evidenced in many Old

Testament characters. The reason for this is that the epistle was written to people who were accustomed to walking by sight according to the types and shadows. They wanted to see with their eyes, and they were reluctant to believe with their hearts what they could not see.

The Divisions of Hebrews

A suggested division to facilitate an organized understanding of Hebrews is as follows:
1. The superiority of Christ as Savior and High Priest (1:1–2:18)
2. The true home of God's people (3:1–4:13)
3. The priesthood of Christ (4:14–7:28)
4. The new covenant (8:1–10:18)
5. Walking by faith (10:19–12:11)
6. Practical exhortations (12:13–25)

Methodology

This is a study guide, not a commentary. It therefore does not primarily take a statement or an explanatory format, but a question format that is intended to help God's people define and understand the teaching of Hebrews. I have deliberately asked the difficult "why" and "how" questions in order to foster an understanding of this scripture. As much as possible, the questions are deliberately leading, interspersed with explanatory remarks, with the goal of encouraging discussion and thoughtful study of Hebrews, whether in Bible study societies or on a personal level. To the extent that the questions are accurately answered, the student of Hebrews will gain an understanding of the epistle.

Suggested Study Resources

Edgar Andrews, *A Glorious High Throne*, Evangelical Press.
    F. F. Bruce, *The Epistle to the Hebrews*, William. B. Eerdmans Publishing Company.
    John Calvin, *Commentary on Hebrews*, William. B. Eerdmans Publishing Company.

Philip E. Hughes, *A Commentary on the Epistle to the Hebrews*, William B. Eerdmans Publishing Company.

Hywel R. Jones, *Let's Study Hebrews*, The Banner of Truth Trust.

Part 1

The Superiority of Christ As Savior and High Priest
Hebrews 1:1–2:18

Hebrews 1:1–3

Without any formal introduction the writer plunges directly into his subject. The point of verses 1–3 is that Christ is superior to the Old Testament prophets.

A clearer translation of verses 1–2a is: "God, who at many times and in many ways spoke to the fathers in the prophets, has in these last days spoken to us in his Son."

1. What are the many times (v. 1)?

2. In what ways did God speak?

3. What is "time past"?

4. Who are the fathers?

5. What was the message of the prophets?

6. What are the last days (v. 2)?

7. What is the difference between God's speech by the prophets and his speech by his Son?

Verses 2b–3 state seven facts that show how Christ is superior to the Old Testament prophets.

8. God has appointed Christ heir of all things. What is included in all things (v. 2)?

9. Through Christ God made the worlds (literally, ages). What are these ages?

10. Christ is the brightness (literally, effulgence) of God's glory. How was God's glory revealed in the Old Testament?

11. Christ is "the express image [*character* or exact impression] of [God's] person" (literally, being or existence) (v. 3). What implications do these descriptions of Christ have for our knowledge of God?

12. Christ upholds all things by the "word of his power." How does his word do this? What doctrine is taught here?

13. Christ has purged (made purification for) sins. How is this work different from the work of the Old Testament priests?

14. Christ is seated at the right hand of the Majesty on high. Why is Christ pictured as being seated? What is the significance of the right hand? What does Christ do while seated?

Hebrews 1:4–14

The premise of these verses is that Christ is superior to the angels, who played a large part in the history of the Old Testament. Christ is made better than the angels. "Better" in Hebrews does not mean qualitatively superior but stronger or more powerful.

1. Who or what are the angels introduced in verse 4? What is their relation to men?

2. What were their functions in the Old Testament?

3. How is Christ better (stronger or more powerful) than the angels?

4. What is Christ's inheritance?

5. What is Christ's name that is better than that of the angels?

The writer shows by seven quotations from the Old Testament that Christ is superior to the angels (vv. 5–14).

6. What is the answer to the first rhetorical question in verse 5? What Old Testament passage does the writer use in this verse? How does this verse differentiate between Christ and the angels?

7. To what Old Testament passage does the second question in verse 5 refer? How does this quotation prove Christ's superiority to the angels?

8. When did God bring his first begotten into the world (v. 6)? To what historical event does the writer refer? In what sense is "first" used? The quotation "And let all the angels of God worship him" is not found in the original Hebrew but is taken from the Greek Septuagint, with reference to Deuteronomy 32:43 and Psalm 97:7. How does this quotation show the superiority of Christ?

9. Where in scripture is the quotation in verse 7 found? Spirits (winds) and fire are transient. How does this quotation imply the superiority of Christ?

10. What Old Testament passage is referred to in verses 8–9?

11. What is the significance of beginning verse 8 with "but"?

12. What is the meaning of God's throne? How does the expression regarding God's throne show Christ's superiority?

13. What is the meaning of a scepter?

14. What is the connection between righteousness and God's kingdom (vv. 8–9)?

15. How does the fact that the scepter of righteousness is the scepter of his kingdom show Christ's superiority?

16. What Old Testament passage is referred to in verses 10–12?

17. How is Christ superior to the creation?

18. How is this proved in verses 11–12a?

19. In what way will the heavens be changed?

20. What contrast is drawn in verse 12b?

21. What attribute of God is taught in verse 12b?

22. What are the scriptural references of the quotations in verses 13–14?

23. What is the implied answer to the question asked in verse 13?

24. How does verse 13 show Christ's superiority to the angels?

25. What is the implied answer to the question in verse 14?

26. What does "ministering" mean? What does this tell us regarding the plan of salvation?

Hebrews 2:1–4

Based on the quotations in chapter 1, the writer in 2:1–4 draws a conclusion. These verses are connected to the previous chapter with "therefore" (2:1).

1. What are the things we have heard (v. 1)?

2. What does the exhortation to "give the more honest heed" mean?

3. What is the reason we must do this?

4. To "let them slip" creates the figure of a drifting and sinking ship. What does it mean to let the things which we have heard slip? The writer now gives reason not to let them slip.

5. What was the word spoken by angels (v. 2)?

6. What does it mean that it was steadfast?

7. What are some examples of how this steadfastness showed itself?

8. How would you answer the question, "How shall we escape, if we neglect so great a salvation" (v. 3)?

9. Why is that salvation great?

10. When did the Lord begin to speak of salvation?

11. Who are those who heard him? Why is their confirmation important?

12. How did God bear witness to the word of the gospel (v. 4)?

13. What are signs?

14. What are wonders?

15. What are miracles?

16. What are the gifts of the Holy Spirit?

17. Why is the phrase "according to his own will" important?

Hebrews 2:5–9

In these verses the superior glory of Christ is compared to the status of the angels.

1. What is "the world to come" (v. 5)?

2. What world is now administered by the angels?

3. What is the "certain place where one testified? What is the point of the questions quoted in verse 6?

4. How does verse 7 answer this question?

5. How is man "a little lower than" or inferior to the angels? What scripture is quoted here?

6. In what way did God crown man with glory and honor?

7. What are the works of God's hands?

8. How is the all-comprehensive subjection of God's handi-works to man emphasized (v. 8)?

9. We do not yet see all things subjected to man. When will we see that?

10. How do we see Jesus (v. 9)?

11. Read 2 Corinthians 5:21. Why was Jesus "made a little lower than the angels" (Heb. 2:9)?

12. What is the meaning of his being "crowned with glory and honour"?

13. What was the way for Jesus to be crowned?

14. Does "every man" in verse 9 imply universal salvation? What is your proof for your answer?

Hebrews 2:10–18

In these verses Christ is pictured as the savior (vv. 10–16) and the high priest (vv. 17–18) of his people. Verse 10 starts with "for," which introduces the idea that Christ's being the savior is the reason for the foregoing verses.

1. Who is the one spoken of in verse 10? What is it that "became him"?

2. What does it mean that all things are for him? That all things are by him?

3. Who are the "many sons"?

4. Who is the "captain of their salvation"?

5. Why is it appropriate that he is made perfect in the way of suffering?

Verses 11–13 teach the unity of the sanctified with Christ.

6. What is sanctification?

7. Who is the sanctifier (v. 11)?

8. Who are the sanctified?

9. What does it mean that the one who sanctifies and the sanctified ones "are all of one"?

10. How does the writer prove the teaching that the sanctified ones are brethren (vv. 12–13)? With whom are they brethren?

11. What Old Testament references are used for that proof?

12. Why is the mention of children in verse 13 important?

Verses 14–16 portray Christ as the deliverer of his people.

13. What is the significance of "flesh and blood" (v. 14)?

14. What truth is taught by the statement that Christ "took part of the same"?

15. Why did Christ have to go through death to destroy the devil?

16. Does the devil have absolute power over death?

17. Who are those who fear death (v. 15)? How is this fear removed?

18. What does it mean to be "subject to bondage"?

19. How did Christ accomplish deliverance—negatively and positively (v. 16)?

In verses 17–18 Christ is described as the high priest of his people.

20. What does it mean that Christ was "made like unto" his brethren (v. 17)? Why was this necessary?

21. What is a high priest? What is his calling? What is his function? What is his character?

22. How is Christ our high priest?

23. What does it mean that he is merciful? Faithful?

24. What are the "things pertaining to God"?

25. What does "reconciliation" mean?

26. How does our high priest make reconciliation?

27. When and how was Christ tempted (v. 18)?

28. Who are those who are tempted?

29. How does Christ succor, or aid, them?

Part 2

The True Home
of God's People
Hebrews 3:1–4:13

Hebrews 3:1–6

The concepts *apostle* and *high priest* are key ideas in Hebrews 3. In verses 1–6 Jesus is pictured as being superior to Moses, the outstanding figure in the Old Testament.

1. In what sense are the writer's brethren holy (v. 1)?

2. What is the "heavenly calling" of which they are partakers?

3. Why should we "consider the apostle and high priest of our profession"?

4. How is Jesus God's apostle?

5. What is our profession?

6. In what way was Jesus faithful (v. 2)? How was Moses faithful?

7. What was Moses' house?

8. What comparison does the writer use to compare the building done by Moses to that of Christ (vv. 3–4)?

9. How is God's building of all things related to Christ (v. 4)?

10. How was Moses faithful in building his house (v. 5)?

11. What are "those things which were to be spoken after"?

12. What was Moses' testimony?

13. What was Moses' relation to God's house?

14. What is Christ's relation to God's house (v. 6)?

15. What is meant by "the confidence and the rejoicing" of our hope to the end?

16. Why is it necessary for us to hold fast this confidence and rejoicing?

Hebrews 3:7–19

In these verses the writer demonstrates that the rejection of Christ is worse than the rejection of Moses, the representative of the Old Testament. He begins this section with *"wherefore,"* by which he indicates that he concludes this from the preceding section, citing the Old Testament with which his readers were familiar.

1. Why does the writer mention the Holy Spirit (v. 7)?

2. From what psalm does the writer quote in these verses? What is the point the writer is making with his use of the psalm?

3. How is it possible to harden one's heart (v. 8)?

4. What is the primary scriptural example of such self-hardening?

5. What is "the provocation"?

6. What history is recalled in verses 9–11?

7. What is "an evil heart of unbelief" (v. 12)?

8. How does this heart reveal itself?

9. How does the writer emphasize the urgency of exhorting one another (v. 13)?

10. What is "the deceitfulness of sin"?

11. How does the deceitfulness of sin harden a person?

12. What is "the beginning of our confidence" (v. 14)?

13. Does the word "if" mean that being partaker of Christ is conditioned on holding the beginning of our confidence?

14. Verse 14 mentions a beginning and an end. What is that end?

15. What was the occasion that caused some to harden their hearts (v. 15)?

16. What Old Testament scripture does the writer use to make his point in verses 15–18?

17. What conclusion is drawn in verse 19?

Hebrews 4:1–10

In verse 1 the writer again uses "therefore" to indicate a conclusion from the preceding section.

1. What is the promise of entering into God's rest (v. 1)?

2. Why should we fear? In what way should we fear?

3. What does it mean to "come short" of the promise?

4. Verse 2 uses two different pronouns—"us" and "them." Who are these two separate groups?

5. What is the gospel?

6. What does it mean for the word to profit people? Why did the gospel not profit one group of people?

7. What is the idea of "rest" (v. 3)?

8. What is the Old Testament reference of verse 3? How does this demonstrate the point of these verses?

9. Why did God swear in his wrath that Israel would not enter his rest?

10. What is the connection between those not entering and the fact that God's works were finished from the foundation of the world?

11. What proof from the Old Testament does the writer give for God's rest (vv. 4–5)?

12. Why must some enter the rest (v. 6)?

13. Who are those who must enter the rest?

14. Who do not enter in? Why do they not enter?

15. What Old Testament reference is used regarding David (v. 7)?

The correct translation of verse 8 is "For if Joshua had given them rest, then would he [David] not afterward have spoken of another day."

16. If Joshua had given them rest, what would have been the consequence (v. 8)?

17. What conclusion does the writer draw in verse 9?

18. Whose rest is meant in verse 10?

19. What does it mean to cease from one's own works?

20. How is this related to entering the rest?

21. What standard is used as proof that one must cease from one's own works?

Hebrews 4:11–13

In verse 11 the writer again uses "therefore" to indicate a conclusion from the preceding verses.

1. How do we labor "to enter into the rest" (v. 11)? Does this make this entering a matter of merit?

2. What warning is given in verse 11?

3. What reason is given in verse 12 for this warning? What is the meaning of the symbolism of the two-edged sword in the verse?

4. In what sense is "word" used in verse 12?

5. What does it mean that the word is quick (alive)?

6. How is it possible to divide soul and spirit, joints and marrow?

7. What does this tell us about the power of the word?

8. How does the word discern "the thoughts and intents of the heart"?

9. What attribute of God is described in verse 13?

Part 3

The Priesthood of Christ
Hebrews 4:14–7:28

Hebrews 4:14–16

Once again the writer draws a conclusion from the foregoing, connecting the ideas with the words "seeing then." In so doing he introduces Christ as our high priest and explains Christ's superiority to the Old Testament priesthood.

1. Who is our high priest (v. 14)? In what way is he great?

2. What does it mean that Jesus is "passed into the heavens"?

3. What does it mean for our high priest to "be touched by the feeling of our infirmities" (v. 15)?

4. Of what comfort is it that our high priest "was in all points tempted [tested] like as we are"?

5. How could he remain without sin?

6. "Therefore" again indicates a conclusion. How is verse 16 the conclusion of verses 14–15?

7. What is mercy? What is grace (v. 16)?

8. How do we "obtain mercy" and "find grace"?

Hebrews 5:1–10

These verses begin the discussion of Christ's priesthood. He is a high priest in four ways.

1. Christ is a sacrificing priest (vv. 1–3).

    a. What is the meaning of the ordination of the high priest (v. 1)?

    b. What was the office and function of the Old Testament high priest?

    c. What are the "things pertaining to God"?

    d. What are the "gifts and sacrifices" offered by the priest?

    e. What is their significance?

    f. Who are those "that are out of the way" (v. 2)?

g. What does it mean that Christ is "compassed [beset] by infirmity" (v. 2)?

h. Verse 3 reveals how there is salvation from this being beset by infirmity. How is that salvation accomplished?

2. Christ is a high priest, being called by God (vv. 4–6).

   a. What is the requirement for being the high priest (v. 4)?

   b. How did Christ come to occupy the high priestly office (v. 5)?

   c. What does his being God's begotten Son have to do with being a high priest?

   d. How is the reference to Melchisedec connected with Christ's office as priest (v. 6)?

3. Christ is a high priest who is diligent in his office (vv. 7–8).

   a. To what incident in Christ's life does verse 7 refer?

   b. What does this incident tell us about Christ's fulfillment of the office of high priest?

c. How or in what way did Christ learn obedience (v. 8)?

d. Why did he have to learn obedience?

e. To whom and to what did he have to learn obedience?

4. Christ is a perfect high priest (vv. 9–10).

   a. How was Christ made perfect (v. 9)?

   b. How was Christ the "author of eternal salvation"?

   c. To whose benefit is this salvation?

   d. How is being made perfect related to Christ's being the author of salvation?

   e. What is the order of Melchisedec (v. 10)?

Hebrews 5:11–14

The writer in these verses finds it difficult to explain the concept of Melchisedec's priesthood (v. 11). He attributes this to the hearers' dull hearing and then expands on this assertion in verses 12–14.

1. How does one manifest that he is "dull of hearing" (v. 11)?

2. Do we know why the addressees had backslidden?

3. What are the "first principles" that they need to be taught again (v. 12)?

4. What are the oracles of God (v. 12)?

5. What is "milk" in the writer's analogy (vv. 12–13)?

6. What is "strong meat" (vv. 12, 14)?

7. What is "the word of righteousness" (v. 13)?

8. What is it to be "unskillful in the word of righteousness"?

9. Using the analogy of a babe, what does the writer say about those who are unskillful in the word?

10. Who are those "of full age" (v. 14)?

11. What is the reason for the expression "by reason of use [of a habit]" (v. 14)?

12. What is it to have the senses exercised?

13. What is the result of this exercise?

Hebrews 6:1–3

Once again the writer transitions with "therefore" to draw a conclusion from the foregoing. He encourages his readers to persevere unto perfection.

1. What are "the principles of the doctrine of Christ" (v. 1)?

2. Why must the believers leave them?

3. What are they not to do?

4. Why must we not lay "again the foundation of repentance from dead works, and of faith"?

5. What is "the doctrine of baptisms" (v. 2)?

6. What is the meaning of the "laying on of hands"?

7. How do the doctrines of resurrection and eternal judgment fit here (v. 3)?

8. Why does the writer add "if God permit"?

Hebrews 6:4–8

These verses describe what is generally called the unforgiveable sin, this being the only one.

1. What is the sin addressed in verses 4–8?

2. What word in verse 4 indicates that the sin is unforgiveable?

3. What is it to be "enlightened"?

4. What is the "heavenly gift"?

5. In what sense do these sinners partake of the Holy Spirit?

6. What is the "good word of God" (v. 5)?

7. What are "the powers of the world to come"?

8. What does it mean that these sinners "have tasted" of these things?

9. What language describes their apostasy (v. 6)?

10. Why is it impossible "to renew them again unto repentance" (vv. 4, 6)?

11. What does it mean to "crucify...the Son of God afresh [again]" (v. 6)?

12. What is it to "put him to an open shame"?

13. What allegory does the writer use in verses 7–8?

14. What effect does the rain have (v. 7)?

15. What is the negative side of this effect (v. 8)?

16. What does the figurative rain symbolize (v. 7)?

17. What do the different effects of the rain symbolize (vv. 7–8)?

Hebrews 6:9–12

In these verses, in contrast to the unforgiveable sin, believers are exhorted to diligence.

1. What are "the things that accompany salvation" (v. 9)?

2. Why is the writer "persuaded [of] better things" regarding the believers (those whom he calls "beloved")?

3. What are the believers' "work and labour of love" (v. 10)?

4. How did they minister to the saints?

5. What does it mean to show "diligence to the full assurance of hope unto the end" (v. 11)?

6. What is the purpose or result of this?

7. What is it to be slothful (v. 12)?

8. Who are those who "inherit the promises"?

9. What are the promises (plural)?

10. What is the relation between faith and patience and inheriting the promises (v. 12)?

Hebrews 6:13–20

These verses strengthen and reinforce the previous admonition to diligence by the example of God's swearing an oath to Abraham.

1. Why did God swear an oath to Abraham (v. 13)?

2. What was the content of the oath (v. 14)?

3. What promise did Abraham obtain (v. 15)?

4. Why is an oath the "end of all strife" (v. 16)?

5. Why was God willing "to shew unto the heirs of promise the immutability of his counsel" (v. 17)?

6. What is the relation between God's counsel and his swearing an oath?

7. What are the "two immutable things" (v. 18)?

8. Why is it "impossible for God to lie"?

9. What is "a strong consolation"?

10. What is "the hope set before us"?

11. How is hope "an anchor of the soul" (v. 19)?

12. What is meant by "within the veil"?

13. How does hope enter "into that within the veil"?

14. How is it possible to enter?

15. How is it possible for Jesus to enter (v. 20)?

Hebrews 7:1–3

In verse 1 Melchisedec is mentioned for the fourth time in the epistle. This time it begins a lengthy comparison between his priesthood and that of Aaron, a discussion that takes up all of chapter 7. How this relates to the priesthood of Jesus will be explained later. The first three verses identify Melchisedec.

1. What does the name "Melchisedec" mean (v. 1)?

2. What does "king of Salem" mean?

3. Why is Melchisedec called "priest of the most high God"?

4. What double office did Melchisedec uniquely hold?

5. What historical incident is referred to in verse 1?

6. What does "King of Salem" mean (v. 2)?

7. In what sense did Melchisedec have neither father nor mother (v. 3)?

8. How could he have "neither beginning of days, nor end of life"?

9. If he is "made like unto the Son of God" and is "a priest continually," is he eternal?

Hebrews 7:4–10

These verses describe the greatness of Melchisedec's priest-hood, especially as it is superior to the Levitical priesthood.

1. How does Abraham's tithing—giving a tenth of the spoils of war-show Melchisedec's lofty position in the Old Testament (v. 4)?

2. What was the significance of Abraham's tithing?

3. What was the "commandment to take tithes of the people" of Israel (v. 5)?

4. What principle is stated in verse 7?

5. What is the significance of the fact that "here men that die receive tithes," while Melchisedec lives and receives tithes (v. 8)?

6. How could Levi and the Levitical priesthood pay tithes to Melchisedec when Levi had not yet been born and the Levitical priesthood had not begun (vv. 9–10)?

Hebrews 7:11–19

In these verses the writer continues his teaching that Aaron's (the Levitical) priesthood was inferior to Melchisedec's; Christ is a priest forever after the order of Melchisedec and not after the order of Aaron.

1. What is the correct answer to the rhetorical question of verse 11?

2. What is the connection between the Levitical priesthood and the law?

3. Who is the other "priest [who] should rise after the order of Melchisedec, and not be called after the order of Aaron"?

4. What was the change of the priesthood? How did that affect the law (v. 12)?

5. Who is the one "of whom these things are spoken" (v. 13)?

6. What tribe is meant in verses 13–14?

7. Why does the writer appeal to Moses in verse 14?

8. What is "far more evident" according to verse 15?

9. What is "the similitude of Melchisedec"?

10. What is "the law of a carnal commandment" (v. 16)?

11. What is "the power of an endless life"?

12. Who is speaking in verse 17, and to whom does he speak?

13. What is "a disannulling of the commandment going before" (v. 18)?

14. In what way is the previous commandment characterized by "weakness and unprofitableness"?

15. Why did not the law make anything perfect (v. 19)?

16. What is the better hope of verse 19?

17. How is this hope the means "by...which we draw nigh unto God"?

Hebrews 7:20–28

These verses picture Jesus as the high priest of a better testament (covenant). This is true because he is a priest after the order of Melchisedec and not according to the Levitical priesthood. Thus Christ is described as a perfect savior.

1. What is the Old Testament reference in verses 20–21?

2. Which priests are meant in verse 21?

3. What is the function of the oath referred to in verses 20–21?

4. What is the surety of verse 22?

5. How was Jesus made this surety?

6. What is the better covenant? Better than what?

7. Why was it necessary to have many priests in the Old Testament (v. 23)?

8. Who is the man in verse 24 with "an unchangeable priesthood"?

9. Why is his priesthood unchangeable?

10. What is the result of his priesthood (v. 25)?

11. How does Jesus save to the uttermost?

12. How is Jesus' perfection described in verse 26?

13. How does this make him an appropriate savior?

14. Why did he not need to offer sacrifices first for himself and then for the people (v. 27)?

15. How does the law make men with infirmities high priests (v. 28)?

16. In what way did the oath come after the law?

17. How does the "word of the oath" make (appoint) the Son?

18. What does it mean that the Son "is consecrated forever"?

Part 4

The New Covenant
Hebrews 8:1–10:18

Hebrews 8:1–6

Verses 1–2 summarize what the writer has previously stated. Verses 3–5 should be regarded as a parenthesis.

1. What is "the throne of the Majesty in the heavens" (v. 1)?

2. What is the meaning of the high priest's sitting "on the right hand" of this throne?

3. What does it mean that the high priest is "a minister of the sanctuary [holy things]" (v. 2)?

4. What is "the true tabernacle, which the Lord pitched"?

5. What are the "gifts and sacrifices" of verse 3?

6. Who is "this man" in verse 3 referring to? What does he have to offer?

7. Why would he not be a priest if he were on earth (v. 4)?

8. How do the priests who offer according to the law serve "unto the example [copy] and shadow of heavenly things" (v. 5)?

9. Why was it necessary for Moses to be very correct in the building of the tabernacle?

10. Resuming the thought of verses 1–2, what is the "more excellent ministry" Jesus has obtained (v. 6)?

11. What is the "better covenant"?

12. What are the "better promises" on which the better covenant was established?

Hebrews 8:7–13

In these verses we find the idea of the new covenant. It is different from the old covenant (vv. 7–9). It is governed by God's law in the heart (v. 10).

1. What is the "first covenant" (v. 7)?

2. In what way was it not faultless? What fault did God find (v. 8)?

3. Through whom does God speak in verses 8–12?

4. What is the "new covenant with the house of Israel" and "of Judah" (v. 8)?

5. What is the covenant described in verse 9?

6. What are "those days" after which God will institute the new covenant (v. 10)?

7. How will God put his "laws into their mind, and write them in their hearts"?

8. What is the essence of the new covenant?

9. How is it different from the old?

10. How will the new covenant manifest itself (vv. 10–11)?

11. How does this differ from the old covenant?

12. Why is the teaching of verse 11 unnecessary under the new covenant (v. 12)?

13. How is being merciful a characteristic of the new covenant?

14. What is the relation between God's being merciful and his not remembering their sins?

15. How does God make the former covenant old, or obsolete (v. 13)?

16. When does the transition from the old to the new occur?

17. In what way does the old covenant "vanish away"?

Hebrews 9:1–5

The first five verses of Hebrews 9 describe the main elements of worship under the first covenant.

1. What were "ordinances of divine service" found in the first covenant (v. 1)?

2. What was the "worldly sanctuary"?

3. What was the significance of the candlestick, table, and showbread in the first tabernacle (v. 2)?

4. What is the meaning "sanctuary"?

5. What was the second veil (v. 3)? What was the first?

6. What was the basic idea of the cherubim (v. 5)?

7. What was the significance of the mercy seat?

8. What in general was the significance and nature of these elements?

Hebrews 9:6–10

These verses describe the function of the priests in the first covenant.

1. When were the elements of the first tabernacle, as described in verses 1–5 ordained, or prepared (v. 6)?

2. What was included in "the service of God" that the priests accomplished?

3. Where did the priests go to do this?

4. Why could only the high priest go into the most holy place (v. 7)?

5. When did he do this?

6. What did he do with the blood?

7. What is "the holiest of all" (v. 8)?

8. Why did the Holy Spirit indicate that the way to it "was not yet made manifest [open]"?

9. What time limit is placed on this?

10. What does it mean that the first tabernacle "was a figure [symbol] for the time" (v. 9)?

11. What was the shortcoming of the "gifts and sacrifices"?

12. What does the conscience have to do with this?

13. When is "the time of reformation" (v. 10)?

Hebrews 9:11–14

These verses describe Christ's eternal redemption in the way of the sacrifice of himself and in contrast to the Old Testament sacrifices.

1. In what way is Christ a "high priest of good things to come" (v. 11)?

2. What is "a greater and more perfect tabernacle"?

3. What is meant by "this building"?

4. Why are "the blood of goats and calves" and "the ashes of a heifer" insufficient for redemption (vv. 12–13)? In contrast, what is sufficient for redemption (v. 12)?

5. What was the effectiveness of the "purifying of the flesh" (v. 13)?

6. What is the point made by the rhetorical question of verses 13–14?

7. What does it mean that Christ offered himself "through the eternal Spirit" (v. 14)?

8. What is the purging of the conscience?

9. Why are works called dead?

Hebrews 9:15–22

These verses describe Christ as the mediator of the new covenant, including the idea of a testament, or covenant.

1. What is the cause that "he is the mediator of the new testament [covenant]" (v. 15)?

2. What were "the transgressions that were under the first testament"?

3. What is the purpose of Jesus' being the mediator of the new covenant?

4. What is the principle stated in verses 16–17?

5. What conclusions does the writer draw in verse 18?

6. Why did Moses speak "every precept to all the people according to the law" (v. 19)?

7. What was the significance of the following items in verse 19:

   a. the blood?

   b. water?

   c. scarlet (purple) wool?

   d. hyssop?

8. Why did Moses sprinkle "almost all things" with blood (vv. 20–22)?

Hebrews 9:23–28

These verses describe Christ's perfect sacrifice that he offered once, in contrast to the many sacrifices of the old covenant.

1. Why was it "necessary that the patterns [copies] of things in the heavens be should purified" with the ceremonies of the old covenant (v. 23)?

2. What are the "better sacrifices" of verse 23?

3. What does it mean that "the holy places made with hands...are the figures of the true" (v. 24)?

4. What is "the true" of which those holy places were figures?

5. Why does Christ "appear in the presence of God for us"?

6. Why could not Christ "offer himself often" (vv. 25–26)?

7. What does it mean that he "put away sin" (v. 26)?

8. What is the analogy of verses 27–28?

9. Who are the "many" of verse 28?

10. What does it mean that Christ will come "the second time without sin"?

Hebrews 10:1–4

These verses make clear the inadequacy of the rites and sacrifices mandated by the law.

1. What are the "good things to come" (v. 1)?

2. What was the shadow that the law had concerning these things?

3. What is the "very image of [these] things"?

4. What is the proof that the sacrifices cannot make perfect those who come and offer (vv. 1–2)?

5. What purpose did the Old Testament sacrifices serve (v. 3)?

6. What principle is expressed in verse 4?

Hebrews 10:5–10

The writer now proves his statements by quoting from Psalm 40:6–8 and from the words of Christ.

1. Who speaks in verses 5–9?

2. Who originally wrote/said these words in Psalm 40?

3. What is the body that has been prepared (v. 5)?

4. What is "the volume of the book" (v. 7)?

5. What is the relation between the sacrifices and doing God's will (vv. 7–9)?

6. How are we sanctified or consecrated (v. 10)?

Hebrews 10:11–18

Verses 11–18 speak of Christ's perfect sacrifice, and verses 14–18 give the result of this atonement.

1. If the same sacrifices were repeatedly administered, but could not take away sin, as verse 11 says, why did the Old Testament church continue to make them?

2. Why is Christ called a man in verse 12?

3. What doctrines are taught in verse 12?

4. What truth is expressed in verse 13?

5. Who are the sanctified (v. 14)?

6. What does it mean that they are perfected?

7. How does the Holy Spirit "witness to us" (v. 15)?

8. Who is speaking in verse 16?

9. What is the content of the covenant that God makes (vv. 16–17)?

10. What conclusion does the writer draw in verse 18?

$\mathcal{P}art\,5$

Walking by Faith
Hebrews 10:19–12:11

Hebrews 10:19–21

Having set forth in the preceding verses the truths of the new covenant and the eternal perfection of believers, the writer now speaks of entry by faith into the most holy place.

1. Remember the constraints of the old covenant under which the Hebrews were used to living. Why is boldness mentioned as being the manner in which believers in the new covenant enter the most holy place (v. 19)?

2. How do believers enter the most holy place?

3. What is "a new and living way" (v. 20)?

4. What does it mean that Christ consecrated, or opened, the way for us?

5. The veil and Christ's flesh are equated in verse 20. In what way is this true?

6. What is "the house of God" (v. 21)?

7. How is Christ a "high priest over the house of God"?

Hebrews 10:22–25

These verses contain three exhortations to the church: let us draw near to God, let us hold fast our faith, and let us not forsake our assembling.

1. What is "a true heart" (v. 22)?

2. How are "a true heart" and the "full assurance of faith" related?

3. What is an evil conscience? What does it mean that "our hearts [are] sprinkled from an evil conscience"?

4. What is the significance of the washing of our bodies "with pure water"?

5. What is "the profession of our faith" (v. 23)?

6. How can we "hold fast" our profession?

7. How do we "consider one another" (v. 24)?

8. How do we "provoke unto love and to good works"?

9. What is the "assembling of ourselves together" (v. 25)? Why is it important? What must we do instead?

10. What is the approaching day?

Hebrews 10:26–31

These verses are introduced by "for," and thus give the reason for what the writer has said in the preceding verses. These verses are a sharp warning against the sin of deliberately rejecting the gospel.

1. What is involved with sinning willfully (v. 26)?

2. What happens to those who "sin wilfully after that [they] have received the knowledge of the truth"?

3. What is the "looking for of judgment" (v. 27)?

4. Who are the adversaries?

5. What is the Old Testament teaching referred to in verse 28?

6. What does the severity of this punishment teach us?

7. What point do the rhetorical questions of verses 28–29 drive home?

8. What does it mean to tread "under foot the Son of God" (v. 29)?

9. What does it mean to count "the blood of the covenant… an unholy [common] thing"?

10. What does it mean to do "despite unto the Spirit of grace"?

11. What does verse 30 teach about vengeance?

Hebrews 10:32–39

These verses comprise a call to perseverance and patience in the face of persecution. The last two verses of the chapter connect these ideas to faith, introducing Hebrews 11.

1. What are the "former days" that the church must remember (v. 32)?

2. What does it mean that the recipients of Hebrews were illuminated?

3. What was the "great fight of afflictions" that they endured?

4. What is "a gazingstock" (v. 33)?

5. In what two ways were the Hebrews persecuted?

6. What does it mean that they "had compassion" on the writer in his bonds or chains (v. 34)?

7. What was the "spoiling of [their] goods"?

8. What motivated the Hebrews in their attitude toward persecution?

9. What conclusions does the writer draw in verse 35?

10. What is required to do God's will and "receive the promise" (v. 36)? What is that promise?

11. Who is the one who will come (v. 37)? When will he come?

12. Is faith referred to in verse 38 objective or subjective?

13. What does it mean to "draw back" (v. 38)? Further, what does it mean to "draw back unto perdition" (v. 39)?

14. How does the writer encourage the church?

Hebrews 11:1–3

In this well-known chapter, faith is first defined in verse 1. Then in verses 2–3 its power is described in a general way.

1. What is the substance (ground or confidence) of all things (v. 1)?

2. What are the "things hoped for"?

3. What is meant by the phrase "the evidence of things not seen"?

4. Who are "the elders" (v. 2)?

5. What is the "good report" they obtained?

6. What is the relation between faith and creation (v. 3)?

7. What are the "things which are seen"?

8. What are the "things which do appear"?

Hebrews 11:4–12

These verses describe how faith is evident in the lives and deeds of the patriarchs named therein.

1. Abel (v. 4)

   a. How was Abel's sacrifice "more excellent" than Cain's?

   b. How does Abel yet speak?

2. Enoch (vv. 5–6)

   a. What does it mean that "God...translated him" (v. 5)?

   b. What general principle is stated in verse 6?

3. Noah (v. 7)

   a. What motivated Noah to build the ark?

   b. How did he "condemn the world"?

4. Abraham (vv. 8–10)

   a. How did Abraham show obedience to God's command (v. 8)?

   b. What does it mean that "he sojourned" (v. 9)?

   c. What was the promise of which Abraham, Isaac, and Jacob were heirs?

   d. Why did Abraham dwell "in tabernacles" (vv. 9–10)?

5. Sarah (vv. 11–12)

   a. How did faith work strength in Sarah (v. 11)?

   b. How was her judging God to be faithful the reason that she had a child when she was past childbearing age?

   c. What was the result of Abraham's and Sarah's faith in God's promise (v. 12)?

Hebrews 11:13–16

These verses relate the attitude toward God's promises on the part of the patriarchs just named in verses 4–12.

1. What does it mean that they "all died in faith" (v. 13)?

2. In what sense did they not receive the promises?

3. What does it mean that they saw the promises afar off?

4. What does their embracing the promises mean?

5. What does it mean to be "strangers and pilgrims on the earth"?

6. What is the implication of being strangers and pilgrims (v. 14)?

7. What does verse 15 tell us about the strength of their faith?

8. What is the country that they seek (v. 16)?

9. What is God's reaction to the strength of their faith?

10. Why do they seek the heavenly city?

Hebrews 11:17–32

In these verses the writer resumes his description of how faith was evident in the lives and deeds of the heroes of faith.

1. Abraham (vv. 17–19)

   a. In what sense did Abraham offer up Isaac (v. 17)?

   b. Why was Abraham's offering such a significant act of faith (v. 18)?

   c. How was Abraham able to obey God's command to sacrifice Isaac (v. 19)?

d. What does it mean that Abraham received Isaac from the dead "in a figure"?

2. Isaac (v. 20)

   a. How did Isaac bless Esau?

   b. What are the "things to come"?

   c. How was Isaac's blessing his sons evidence of his faith?

3. Jacob (v. 21)

   a. How was Jacob's blessing similar to Isaac's? How was it different?

   b. Jacob "blessed both the sons of Joseph." How was that evidence of his faith?

4. Joseph (v. 22)

   a. How was Joseph's mentioning the exodus evidence of his faith?

   b. How did his commandment concerning his bones demonstrate his faith?

5. Moses' parents (v. 23)

   a. Who were Moses' parents?

   b. Why did they hide Moses for three months?

   c. What was their attitude toward Egypt and its king?

6. Moses (vv. 24–28)

   a. How was Moses' choice evidence of his faith (vv. 24–25)?

   b. What is "the reproach of Christ" (v. 26)? Does this imply that Moses had a knowledge of Christ?

   c. Why did Moses make this choice?

   d. What is the history of verse 27?

   e. Why was his forsaking Egypt an act of faith (v. 27)?

   f. How did Moses' leadership in celebrating the passover demonstrate his faith (v. 28)?

7. Israel at the Red Sea (v. 29)

   a. What is the history of the Red Sea crossing?

   b. Why was faith required for Israel to pass through the Red Sea?

8. Israel at Jericho (v. 30)

   a. How was Israel's faith demonstrated in the history of the fall of Jericho?

   b. How did faith make "the walls of Jericho [fall] down"?

9. Rahab (v. 31)

   a. What is the history of Rahab?

   b. How were her actions a matter of faith?

10. Various heroes of faith (v. 32). What outstanding deeds of faith were manifest in the lives of:

   a. Gideon

   b. Barak

c. Samson

d. Jepthah

e. David

f. Samuel

g. The prophets

11. Why are many others left out of this list?

Hebrews 11:33–40

Verses 33–38 contain a long list of deeds that God's Old Testament people performed by the power of faith.

1. Find instances in the history of the church of each of the items mentioned in these verses.

2. What does it mean that all those mentioned in verses 33–38 "obtained a good report" (v. 39)?

3. Why did they "receive not the promise" (v. 39)?

4. What does it mean that the Old Testament saints are not made perfect "without us" (v. 40)?

Hebrews 12:1–2

These verses are a summary and application of chapter 11.

1. What is the race that we must run (v. 1)?

2. What is the idea or function of a witness?

3. How is the great "cloud of witnesses" an incentive for us to run our race?

4. How are we able to run this race?

5. What does it mean that Jesus is "the author and finisher of our faith" (v. 2)?

6. How are Jesus' cross and shame his incentive to suffer?

7. How is verse 2 the incentive for verse 1?

Hebrews 12:3–4

These verses describe the opposition to Christ and to the church.

1. What is the "contradiction of sinners" (v. 3)?

2. How is this an incentive not to "be wearied and faint"?

3. What does it mean to resist "unto blood" (v. 4)?

4. What is "striving against sin"?

Hebrews 12:5–11

These verses describe the suffering of Christians as chastening by God.

1. What does it mean that the readers "have forgotten the exhortation" regarding chastening (v. 5)?

2. Do we know how the writer can allege that his readers had forgotten this exhortation?

3. What is chastening? What is the difference between chastening and punishment?

4. What is the reference of the quotation in verse 5–6?

5. What is the relation between God's love and his chastening (v. 6)?

6. If we "endure chastening," what conclusion can we draw (v. 7)?

7. How is the opposite true (v. 8)?

8. What comparison is drawn in verse 9?

9. What does it mean that our earthly fathers "chastened us after their pleasure" (v. 10)?

10. What does it mean that God chastens us "for our profit"?

11. What is the purpose of this chastening?

12. What is the experience of one who is chastened as it is occurring (v. 11)?

13. What is the long-term result of chastening?

14. What is "the peaceable fruit of righteousness"?

Part 6

Practical
Exhortations
Hebrews 12:12–13:25

Hebrews 12:12–13

Hebrews 12:12 begins the practical section of the epistle. These exhortations are based on the foundation of truth established in the entire book to this point. Based on the truth of chastening is the admonition to walk in straight paths.

1. What are the figures of lifting "up the hands which hang down, and the feeble knees" (v. 12)?

2. What are "straight [even] paths" (v. 13)?

3. What is the necessity of walking in the straight paths?

4. What is the alternative?

Hebrews 12:14–17

The main admonition in these verses is to follow peace and holiness. The writer strengthens his point with three warnings.

1. How do we "follow peace…and holiness" "with all men" (v. 14)?

2. What is it to "see the Lord"?

3. Why are peace and holiness indispensable for seeing the Lord?

4. In the first warning of verse 15, what does it mean to "fail of [fall from] the grace of God"?

5. In the second warning of verse 15, what is the "root of bitterness" that springs up?

6. How will this trouble believers?

7. What will be the consequence if the root of bitterness does spring up?

8. How does the history of Esau illuminate the warning found in verse 16?

9. Does verse 17 mean that Esau sincerely sought repentance? Why or why not?

Hebrews 12:18–24

These verses describe the old and new covenants in summary form.

1. What is the historical allusion in verses 18–21? Where did that take place?

2. What is the picture drawn of the old covenant in verses 18–19?

3. How strict was God in instituting the old covenant (vv. 20–21)?

4. What is the difference between Mount Zion (v. 22) and "the mount that might not be touched" from verses 18–21?

5. To what is the church come (vv. 22–24)?

6. Mount Zion is described many different ways in verses 22–24. What do the various descriptions mean?

   a. "the city of the living God" (v. 22)

   b. "the heavenly Jerusalem"

   c. "an innumerable company of angels"

d. "the general assembly and church of the firstborn" (v. 23)

e. "God the Judge of all"

f. "the spirits of just men made perfect"

g. "Jesus the mediator of the new covenant" (v. 24)

h. "the blood of sprinkling"

7. How does "the blood of sprinkling" speak "better things than that of Abel"?

Hebrews 12:25–27

These verses describe the shaking of the heavens and the one who shakes them. The admonition is to refuse not the one who speaks.

1. Who is the one who speaks on earth (v. 25)? From heaven?

2. When did his voice shake the earth (v. 26)?

3. What will be included in the second shaking (vv. 26–27)?

4. When will his promise spoken in verse 26 be fulfilled?

5. What is the "removing of those things that are shaken" (v. 27)?

6. What are the things that "cannot be shaken"?

Hebrews 12:28–29

In contrast to the shaking of verses 25–27, these verses speak of the unshakeable kingdom of God.

1. What is the kingdom we receive (v. 28)?

2. What does it mean that the kingdom "cannot be moved"?

3. What does it mean to "have grace [hold fast]"?

4. What are "reverence and godly fear"?

5. The reason for verse 28 is that God is a consuming fire (v. 29). How is this true?

Hebrews 13:1–6

The theme of these verses is love—of the brethren, of strangers, of prisoners, in sex, and of the neighbor in our walk of life.

1. What is included in "brotherly love" (v. 1)?

2. How should we "entertain strangers" (v. 2)?

3. Why should we entertain strangers?

4. What does it mean to remember those who are in prison (v. 3)?

5. Who are those who are in adversity?

6. Why must we "remember them that are in bonds" and "them which suffer adversity"? What is the body?

7. What is the honorable nature of marriage and the undefiled bed (v. 4)?

8. What is the result of the violation of marriage and the undefiled bed? What does this say about the nature of society today?

9. What is our conversation (v. 5)? What is covetousness?

10. What is God's promise concerning contentment?

11. What other assurance do we have (v. 6)?

Hebrews 13:7–9

For the second time in chapter 13 (see verse 3) we are here admonished to remember. These verses exhort us concerning the leaders of the church.

1. Who are those who "have the rule" and how should we remember them (v. 7)?

2. Why should we follow the faith of those who have spoken to us the word of God?

3. What is the end of their conversation?

4. What benefit do we obtain by "considering the end of their conversation"?

5. How is the immutability of Christ in verse 8 connected with the admonition of verse 7?

6. What is the opposite of verse 8 (v. 9)?

7. What are "divers and strange doctrines"?

8. What is the establishment of the heart?

9. How does grace establish the heart?

10. What are unprofitable meats?

Hebrews 13:10–14

These verses use the idea of sacrifice in a twofold sense—literal and figurative—once more to contrast the old and new covenants.

1. What is the altar that we have (v. 10)?

2. What is the tabernacle?

3. Why do those who serve the tabernacle have no right to eat from our altar?

4. Explain the significance of the sacrifices of verse 11?

5. How was Jesus the fulfillment of these sacrifices (v. 12)?

6. What conclusion does the writer draw in verse 13?

7. How do we bear Jesus' reproach?

8. What reason does the writer give for the exhortation of verse 13 (v. 14)?

Hebrews 13:15–19

Continuing the figure of sacrifice, these verses teach the sacrifice of praise, good works, obedience, and prayer.

1. In what way can we and do we "offer the sacrifice of praise" (v. 15)?

2. How is praise a sacrifice?

3. In what ways, according to verse 16, must we communicate (share)?

4. What is the possibility of doing good works?

5. Who are those who "have the rule" (v. 17)?

6. How, why, and when must they "give account" for our souls?

7. How would a poor report be unprofitable?

8. Who are the plural "we" and "us" in verse 18?

9. What is our conscience?

10. How are the conscience and the desire to live honestly related?

11. Especially for what must the church pray (v. 19)? Why?

12. Does this verse give us a clue concerning the writer's identity? See also 13:23–24.

Hebrews 13:20–21

These verses are the writer's inspired and apostolic blessing on the church.

1. What is the connection between God as "the God of peace" and the God who raised Christ from the dead (v. 20)?

2. Why is God called the "great shepherd of the sheep"?

3. Why is the covenant called everlasting?

4. How is it possible for us to do God's will (v. 21)?

5. What is "well-pleasing in [God's] sight"?

Hebrews 13:22–25

These concluding verses contain admonitions and greetings.

1. What does it mean to suffer (bear with) the exhortations in this epistle (v. 22)?

2. What is the implication of a letter of "few words"?

3. What plans does the writer have (v. 23)?

4. Who must be greeted (v. 24)? Why?

5. What is the writer's likely location?

Conclusion

Grace be with you all. Amen.

Notes

Notes

Notes

Notes

Notes

Notes

Notes

Notes

www.ingramcontent.com/pod-product-compliance
Lightning Source LLC
Chambersburg PA
CBHW071826020426
42331CB00007B/1615